My Prophecies from Morning Revival

Elaine Day

Grosvenor House
Publishing Limited

All rights reserved
Copyright © Elaine Day, 2015

The right of Elaine Day to be identified as the author of this
work has been asserted by her in accordance with Section 78
of the Copyright, Designs and Patents Act 1988

The book cover picture is copyright to Inmagine Corp LLC

This book is published by
Grosvenor House Publishing Ltd
28-30 High Street, Guildford, Surrey, GU1 3EL.
www.grosvenorhousepublishing.co.uk

This book is sold subject to the conditions that it shall not, by way of
trade or otherwise, be lent, resold, hired out or otherwise circulated
without the author's or publisher's prior consent in any form of binding or
cover other than that in which it is published and
without a similar condition including this condition being imposed
on the subsequent purchaser.

A CIP record for this book
is available from the British Library

ISBN 978-1-78148-892-8

Introduction

This is a book on my prophecies after reading on a daily basis the Morning Revival of Witness Lee.

I attend a Recovery Church, which is held in a village near to my home.

I have been attending for some years now, and the fellowship, meetings and home groups and prayer meetings in our homes are very enjoyable.

This therefore is just my thoughts on each weeks reading.

We read what we have understood on Lord's Day, and each day of the week there is a Section for the day to understand and to take in.

Your thoughts on each Prophecy may be different to mine, but I find the time reading alone very rewarding.

The book I read from is called 'The Holy Word for Morning Revival.'

I hope that you enjoy reading through, and you have enjoyment from what I've concluded for each Prophecy.

Elaine Day.

The Vision of Consecration

The burnt offering typifies Christ not mainly in his redeeming man from Sin, but in his living a life that is perfect and absolutely just for God, and God's satisfaction.

The burnt offering is God's food so that God may enjoy it, and that it will satisfy God, a satisfying fragrance to Jehovah.

This was to be made twice daily, in the morning and evening.

To satisfy God we offer a burnt offering in respect to God, a fragrance well pleasing to God, which brings satisfaction, peace, rest.

God needs his people to be clean, righteous, faithful. God hates death much more than Sin.

Death is everywhere, society is filled with the germs of death.

These germs are also in our Church life, so we need to pray daily, hourly, fighting death, the last enemy of God.

The Vision of the Self

We should all deny the self, pick up our cross, and follow Lord Jesus.

Christ is our person for the Church life, as in the living of the One New Man.

This should be carried out in the Spirit.

The Spirit applies the death of Christ.

The self is our soul life with emphasis on human thoughts and human opinions.

We discover this in the Bible where the self is clearly mentioned.

The self is something of Satan in the soul expressed most of the time.

Through opinions, our self is so living active and aggressive, we need to apply the Cross of Lord Jesus every day.

The Vision of the Church

The Body of Christ

The desire of the church in God's desire, a desire of God is to have the Church in this age.

We then need to see the vision of the body.

God is born into our Spirit, which is the centre of our being.

God's desire then is to spread from our Spirit to transform all parts of our soul and eventually to transfigure our physical body.

This will saturate and permeate with the essence of God himself. This is real holiness.

The Vision of Christ

Colossians 2: 17 is the substance and like the shadow of a man's body, the rituals in law are a shadow of Christ, who is the substance, reality of the gospel.

Jesus is the head of the body, thus, to hold the head is simply to enjoy Christ as the reality of all positive things and the more we love other members of the body.

Every day we need Christ, all positive things, in our daily life, must be Christ.

Christ should be our completion, our rest, our beginning, our enjoyment Food, drink, and our satisfaction.

The freshness and newness is Christ as the air we breathe in.

When we turn to our spirit, we must be willing to.

Learn to turn to the Spirit.

The Governing and Controlling Vision – The Vision of God's Economy

When we see the Heavenly vision and it comes into our being the vision will have a powerful and a lasting effect on each of us so we need to become people with a vision. A vision is a special scene, and God's Revelation is a scene.

Revelation as in the heavenly vision will always have a powerful and a lasting effect on us.

This vision captures us, governs us, restricts us, and preserves us, and gives us the boldness to go on.

We need to obey the vision of Jesus as our life, never allowing us to be distracted by doctrines nor strive after good behaviour.

The Church, the embodiment of the Son, takes in his riches, and thus becomes his fullness.

Christ enters into us, and becomes our life.

Bethel – House of God

We need to be fully saturated that in this Universe God is doing one thing – building His Eternal habitation.

The dream that Jacob had at Bethel is crucial in the revelation of God including all the Bible and the need for the rest of the bible to explain it.

In Genesis 35 the vision of Bethel comes again. It came as a dream the first time and the second time a reality, so we need to have both the Dream and the Reality, as the dream is a true picture, and the reality is the same as the dream.

We need to be built up as Christians in the divine life, and for each of us to pursue Christ into his Eternal Economy.

We all need the Christian Life of God, to be built up, strengthened with his building Of Bethel, then we can come into a reality that our all sufficient God is for the building of God's home, and ours.

God needs our bodies to fully function within us, to build us from the inside out, replenish all of us with knowledge and understanding that God is always there for us.

The Lamb as the Lamp With God as the Light

Within the City, there is the Life, but outside there is only the Shining.

The World is in the Shining, but not the Life.

The Life is in the City, and Life is God himself imparted into all his Children.

The Life of God comes into us through the Shining.

Confusion is subdued, and all things are brought to order.

If God never shone, we could never see God's golden divine nature, because we are under the shining of the son as embodiment of God's divine riches, we can then enjoy these riches.

The Triune God is the Lamp Light, and God shines within us through the Lamp.

The Vision of the World

The Greek word for World denotes an order, a set form, an orderly Arrangement, hence, an ordered system (set up by Satan) the adversary of God, not the Earth, the world is an Evil system arranged systematically by Satan.

According to the Bible, the world is against the Father, the Devil against The Son, and the flesh is against the Spirit.

On one hand we have the Divine Trinity, the Father, Son, and Spirit, and on the other hand we have an Evil Trinity, the World, Satan, and it's flesh, We should enjoy the Divine Trinity and have nothing to do with the Evil Trinity.

The Intrinsic Significance of the Name New Jerusalem and the Dimensions of the Holy City

When we have no God, we have no heart.

With God we have Newness, and to be in Newness with God is Divine.

When we are baptized into the Father, Son, Holy Spirit, we enter into the Holy City.

Of the three Holy of Holies we can live and walk in the presence of God.

The Three Holy of Holies are in Exodus, 1 Kings, Revelation.

In our Church life we must be in the Holy of Holies for those who fully believe in God will see, touch, worship, and serve God and will dwell and live in the presence of God.

The Church must be utterly holy.

When we take Christ as our Passover lamb, we take him as a substitute for the beginning of a new sinless life.

The God of Abraham Seen in His Dealings with Abraham

Christ in resurrection germinated a seed into us to make us his new Creation and a New Man.

God is all-sufficient as also is The New Testament.

Abraham walked with God, and spoke to God as one human to another.

God of Abraham is also the God of friendship. God is our shield our Great Reward, and our Justifier.

God was in Harmony with Abraham, he was acceptable to God.

Christ on the Cross was termination of life, and his resurrection germinated life into us.

Two Wells – Two Sources of Living

The Living Water we drink is not natural, it is redeemed at the cost of Christ's full Redemption.

We have two sources of living. One the natural source in the wilderness of our Soul.

The other is the redeemed source in the garden of our Spirit.

Paul said we are to drink one Spirit, this is, one well of water.

The Well at Beer-Sheba is a seed of the New Covenant.

Do you live like Ishmael or Isaac?

Living a Grace – Enjoying Life for God's Good Pleasure.

We approach the Throne of Grace by turning to our Spirit.

When we enthrone Lord Jesus within us, the Spirit as the water of life will flow from the throne to supply each of us.

The enjoyment of our inheritance with Jesus must be through Grace.

God's throne is the living grace.

Our Spirit is only the place where we can receive Grace.

God needs to get into each of us, visit, love one another and even love others for us.

Without Jesus, we are nothing.

Grace is the divine person of the Triune God.

The Allegory of the Two Women

When we do anything for ourselves, it is not by the Grace of God, but when we do anything by God, it is Grace which is defined in the Bible which is specific as God works into each of us.

We should all reach a point in our life where we can say:- I want to do your will, to God.

When you stop working in your natural life, God can then enter into you to guide you, because the blessed are those who stop to listen, then God enters into each of us.

When we enter the New Covenant we enter into the New Jerusalem because the New Jerusalem is the new covenant

Enjoying Christ in His Heavenly Ministry By Fighting for the Brother

We should never separate ourselves from God's Goal. Because God's goal is to be inside each of us. God does not want us to be like Lot, to move as far as possible from him, God needs us to be under his Sovereignty. Christ brings peace between us and God. Peace is necessary for God's building and for His Glory, and God's house is always in peace. Our High Priest brings to us bread and wine to have a good time with us. The Christian life is to slaughter our enemies during the day and to enjoy the Ministry of Jesus with Bread and Wine in the evening. Christ's ministry is in two sections, one on Earth, one in Heaven, Christ has the power to rule over the Earth, and to manage our affairs. Christ prays for us and he always guides us.

The Land for the Fulfilment of God's Purpose

The land for us today is to live in Christ and into whom we are living. The land symbolises Christ, for his habitation & expression & representation. God's people harvest on the land & where God can defeat His enemies. We need to pray 'Lord be in our Spirit.' Doing this we must live, move & behave in the Spirit of Jesus. We receive the Spirit as the blessing of the Gospel. The Spirit in Galatians denotes the Triune God. Before coming to Church, we could not defeat our enemies, but with Christ, and in the Indwelling Spirit, many of our Enemies can be defeated.

The Seed for the Fulfilment of God's Purpose

God's justification is for a reproduction of Christ in Saints. Saints then become the reproduction of Christ and to be a member of the Body of Christ. Abraham believed that God worked something into him to bring forth a seed out of him being for the fulfilment of God's purpose. The faith Abraham had for God is precious to God, and Abraham was justified to have such faith in God. God is our shield, our great reward, and our justifier. God justified Abraham because God was pleased with Abraham, and he was acceptable to God, and had no problem with God. Only what God works into us will be grace and the grace of God will always be with us and is not in vain and is always inside you. Christ redeems us out of a curse. He became a curse on our behalf and was abandoned by God but Christ worked into us bringing us out of a curse, and gave us Salvation.

Living by Faith – Being Today's River Crossers to Live the Life of the Altar and the Tent

We need to leave the outer court where the altar is, and cross over to the Holiest of all, where God is, to leave our soul and to enter into the maturity of life in the truth.

To be saved is to be called to fulfil God's purpose. We can then be delivered out of many negative situations including gossip, and eventually go to God's goal. God's goal is Christ. So we should be in Christ.

We can still lose our vision if we do not live in a continuous way with God appearing to us. But many have no vision of God, or of their calling to God.

We can pray for our selfish thoughts, and end with a definite goal in God's calling, so our salvation is to fill this goal.

There can be an appearing of the living Christ and it should transfuse Christ into each of us.

We are only here on Earth for God, never for ourselves.

Knowing & Experiencing the God of Abraham, the God of Isaac, & the God of Jacob to become the Israel of God.

God is the initiator for everybody, when the Lord guides each of us, he leads the way, not ourselves. When we receive it is the Lord who guides our actions, never ourselves.

We need to be torn apart to receive Lord Jesus, by the Holy Spirit. So that Lord Jesus can build each of us up to a New Man and to listen, learn, and respect him.

(Kai in Greek), means 'even' which means that many individual followers of God become collectively the household and the members of a divine family into the house of the God of Israel.

When anybody says that the church is God, Our father, & Jesus Christ, it becomes much deeper, profound, & a declaration to each person & God Can work into each of us in his Divine Spirit, redeem us from our wicked ways, and nourish us with Love, Understanding, Compassion & germinate us into his New creation.

He can destroy Satan in Death forevermore, place life into each of us, and as the Triune God, three in one, an internal flame within us which never dies but fires us up with the warmth, & Love of the Lord Jesus.

Christ's Heavenly Priesthood Ministered to the Churches for the Producing of the Overcomers

We need to humble ourselves before God as God can then exercise his Heavenly Ministry to supply those who are seeking for the riches of Heaven and the Divine Life. We need Ministry as then Lord Jesus can save all of us to the Uppermost.

As Overcomers we go towards God and sit in his presence. When we do not have Jesus as our daily portion in our Church Life, we would lose enjoyment of Jesus in our daily life.

If we did corrupt Christianity under the influence of Babylon, we would lose our faithfulness and will miss our proper goal, but we do need to burn and infuse others and not to be lukewarm or cold towards others.

The Vision of the Glorious Christ

In order to nourish others with Christ we first seek Christ, experience Christ, gain and enjoy Christ and participate in Christ.

To cherish others is to make them happy, pleasant and comfortable. We must be pleasant on contacting people or we cannot cherish them and make them happy.

In Christ's divinity he nourishes us with himself as the All Inclusive Christ in the Ministry of three stages. In Divinity Christ is nourishing so we can grow and mature in divine life to be Christ's overcomers and to accomplish Christ's Eternal Economy.

God's 'Flame of Fire' is far observing and searching, and his eyes infuse us with all that he sees.

Once Christ looks at you, we could never be cold or aloof as we once were as by looking at us Christ starts to bum inside us and stirs us up to the Lord.

The Shepherding of Christ for the Church As the One Flock and the Father's House

In one sense we are nobody and vain. In another sense we are all wonderful, caring and feeding the sheep of God, so God can then also enter into these lost sheep and restore them and build them up into a wholeness.

We need to flock together to receive God's Zoe life through redemption from the shepherd so that we all can receive Him as the Zoe life, and in the Divine life we can all become one and dwell forevermore with Lord Jesus.

We are sheep for Christ, and Christ is our shepherd so we become one flock that Christ feeds for his Divine and Zoe life.

When we are just a ewe or a ram standing alone, Jesus takes you gently back to the flock so each of us is never lonely.

We are now on commission to nourish, feed, blend, pray for each other, but each sheep that God is preparing for his companionship eventually in Heaven as his Bride will wholly be one in the Heavens and Divine and Zoe life will be ours forevermore.

The Revelation of the Triune God and of the Consummated Spirit

The Lord's Holy Spirit into each of us comes as a comforter into each of us.

Christ in resurrection that is before his Glorification and Spirit being his Divine element gives to us his humanity and reassurance.

We are joined to the Triune Spirit, as a complete and whole being who enters into the Heavens as an eternal human to be with the Lord Jesus as His companion, friend, counterpart.

Jesus being flesh, bringing Grace and reality into each human on earth.

He gives to each of us our expression, kindness, and in the Heavens we are consumed into his grace and reality forevermore.

The Mending Ministry of Life.

Christ died in the form of a grain of wheat so his Divine life can be imparted into each of us.

We are children of God, those who believe in his name are part of God.

Christ was alone, until he died then many grains sprang up.

We need to be broken and ground into fine flour so we can blend with others to make a loaf.

This loaf is the body of Christ which consummates in the New Jerusalem.

We can give to each other life. We impart Christ into each other and his teachings.

But when we sin, we do not have life with the Lord and we are empty vessels.

One person can fully overcome sin, and this is Lord Jesus.

The Church today is the mending ministry of life and in this we experience Christ as our life, and as our whole being.

A Full-grown Corporate Man Fulfilling God's Purpose Through the Experience of Life in the Fourth Stage

God needs man to express himself and to make us into the new man when God perfects us, we will then see the Lord's coming.

We will then be the bride of Christ and we all need this vision to become clearer in our walk with God.

God has a twofold purpose for his redeemed ones, first that we should be filled with God and second we learn to fight for him and to deal with Satan so that the second purpose can be fulfilled in us.

God's image in us is for his expression.

Noah – the Life and Work that Can Change the Age

We need to build our own ark, to walk in with the animals, but to go to the top of the ark where there is Christ, and the window going to heaven so we can be with him, and to work out our own Salvation with Christ, and on this level we can have a deep and a very valuable intimacy with Christ.

To build our Church, we need God.

To abide in Christ, we need to build up in our walk with Christ.

Noah was under God, and we are also under God who cares and loves us, and our testimony will be Jesus who saved us all from our sins and our evil thoughts and our evil doings.

The Tree of Life, and the Tree of the Knowledge of Good and Evil

If we live by the glory of God, God will transfuse and infuse each of us enabling us to live by the faith of God just as Abraham walked with God.

God wants us to reach out to him, to touch him, and to receive life, from Him, to feed us every day, to protect us, and uphold us.

We should only touch the tree of life, as the Tree of Knowledge brings in Satan and his evil ways.

Lord Jesus is the vine, as the Tree of Life grows both sides of the river.

Through Jesus who was crucified, resurrected and came back to give us life, we are the creation of God, and bear witness to his Holy Word.

The Central Thought of God

The Church is very similar to a farm to grow Christ. Each produce grown on the farm is Christ as the farm gives many different aspects of Christ. The Church grows Christ, and it builds the genuine foundation stone for every Saint to eat Christ. Jesus gave up his life so that we could be cleansed by the washing of the Holy Water in the name of Jesus Christ. God within Christ is the Spirit of life and we are the vessels made with a Spirit and we are an inner recipient to receive Lord Jesus. God in Christ is the Spirit is the Tree of Life, real food for Saints to eat and to enjoy. The flowing living water washes within us and this will transform us from clay into precious materials. Christ needs to be increased within us, until we arrive at the fullness of God. This is the real building of the Lord Jesus Christ.

Christ as Everything for the Building of the Temple of God.

To have Christ we need to be cleansed, then to receive his faith and love, which is his to give and his alone, not ours. We can be rooted and then be built in his love, so we can live as Jesus intended us to do, when he created us, gave us life, so we could have a life with wisdom and sanctification, redemption from our sins, and to rise to his Heavenly Kingdom, into the Glory and by the side of Lord Jesus.

Zechariah saw Jesus related to the recovery of God, he had many visions, he was a Priest, who spread his prophecies of the people of Israel,

The Lord Jesus is our portion, our spiritual food, drink, and our constant supply in the Breath, Waking, Talking of the Lord Jesus.

We need to be more in Prophecy like Zechariah, to have visions which we can see clearly, and to be free from being captive from Satan's grasp.

Jesus was a Physician, not a Judge. We therefore should not judge one another, but to feed each other with the love of Jesus, and to show our humanity and warmth, in the way Jesus taught the overcomers.

A praying church in the unique stream of the work of God

In the book of Acts, the apostles prayed before working. We should always pray to God for His answer to all his work.

God chooses his people, who are his Chosen ones, to have the heavenly vision, to be at peace with him for all eternity, to have God's grace, but not whole wisdom as God even after our passing and resurrection will always be above each of us.

We should pray for our Brothers and our Sisters, never gossip, never abuse any of them as God knows their worries, and we can help by prayers and to forgive those who do gossip as Jesus forgave those who acted with Satan inside them, not God.

To gossip is Satan, to pray is the Lord Jesus.

The Vision of the Seventy Weeks and the Age of Mystery

The iron in the feet of the image is solid and communism is like this, but God has a way to make the image soft and to weaken the image and crush it. To be weak and humble and to be at ease with God.

The destiny of Christ as a stone is to crush the great human image and in the crucifixion of Jesus, God cut Jesus into three. The resurrection of Jesus, God made him into a cornerstone, a foundation stone, and a stumbling stone. The stumbling stone was for the Jews who were unbelieving.

We should let Jesus know how much we love him, and for Jesus to appear in our everyday life, he will come with a crown of righteousness, as he is the king of the overseers, and we will be rewarded in the kingdom of heaven.

On Jesus coming we will ask him questions, and Jesus will demand certain things from us, as we wait for the arrival of Jesus, like a slave waiting for our master.

Praying at the Incense Altar for the Formation Of an Army to Fight for God's Move on Earth

The Lord Jesus wants to express himself in each of us, with no limitations, but to place his Spirit into each of us, so he can grow and mould each of us with the divine love he has for each of us.

The incense altar is the divine centre, the heart of God's operation, and with our prayers we go to the Corporate Christ.

Many of us are weak in Spirit, and we need to be strong to build up an army for God.

Spiritual warfare is waged in the air, so to fight this we need to be in the Heaven's with Christ.

The Vision of the Golden Lampstand and the Two Olive Trees

We can be like an Olive Tree which pours out oil, so we can be flowing out Jesus from ourselves into the unsaved. We can then minister Christ in our pouring of oil into others.

We have Grace when we enjoy God.

From the Olive Tree, we can also pour the Oil into the lampstands to shine light, and the burning element to shine God in his Trinity.

Christ is the building stone which has seven eyes, and Christ is the Redeeming Lamb.

Both are one, and the stone and Lamb are always watching over us with seven eyes.

We carry out our daily life with the seven eyes of Christ watching over us and the seven spirits of God.

The number seven is to impart the divine life into us from the flowing of Oil from the Olive Tree, and to pour Gold into a pure Golden Lampstand to shine around the Earth.

A Pattern of a Person Used by God to Turn the Age

The man-child who is Jesus, shepherds the nations, and the man-child Jesus is called to God and to the throne God places a seed in every woman, which is Jesus to cast down Satan and to bruise him.

For God to make a dispensational move towards us, helps us to be closer to his Kingdom, as the Christians who will eventually wear the robes of Linen, Gold, Silver and to be washed by the cleansing of the corporate Christ, from the inside to the outside, taking away our sins, imperfections and preparing us for the New Jerusalem, and to be with the Lord Jesus in the Kingdom.

God needs us as his instruments, as his overcomers, to work inside us, and to nourish us with his love and his Spirit, to be inside us as the Living God, which is one of the dispensational moves working inside of us.

Being One with the Triune God in the Move Of the Great Wheel of His Economy

When we move, it is with the Lord within us. We move within a large wheel, which is made by God. We are the spokes which branch out towards the unsaved, collecting those in need of God, and bringing them within the wheel so God can work his way into them.

We have wheels which take us off in all directions, spreading the Lord where ever we go and having the Lord within us to help with his words.

We should be at one with God, in his move, and in the great economy of his wheel, need to spread God's words.

We have no centre without the Lord, and without the Lord, there is no rim to the wheel, the rim is God and the church, and the counterpart of Jesus.

Persevering in Prayer

When we pray, we breathe and live spiritually with Christ.

To pray is to persevere, because being negative and not at one with the Lord is to argue, and to be bitter with each other.

To pray involves a battle and a fight, but not with each other, but between us and Satan.

We all suffer many failures in our prayers, but we should persevere our prayers, because it is our link to Jesus and his love.

We are heavenly ambassadors on earth when we pray a river flows within us and supplies us. Grace in prayer is more important than having a prayer answered.

We should make a vow to God to be praying people.

We would be enriched and uplifted and enjoy the Lord more.

The more we pray, the more thirsty we become to pray.

We talk to Jesus through our prayers. We breathe so we can have him live in us.

The Priesthood and the Kingship for the Building Up of the Church as the Temple of God

We go through life with our problems, but we call upon Jesus to wash through us as the living water. We receive unspeakable peace, and we are filled with his love. We can enter into the Holy of Holies and then touch the throne.

Mercy and Grace come from God to fill us with peace, when we are feeling low, and we feel what problems remain or may become worse, but with Jesus we have an inner peace to soothe us.

God needs to have his dominion in man, so he can mould us into priests for the Kingdom and on earth to represent God and to be a comfort to others when the wolves enter.

We need to be God's image, to express him, to have our dwelling place open to others, so God can bless each home with his humanity and warmth.

Living in the Fellowship of the Divine Life

Our fellowship with one another cannot be thorough and obstacles will always remain until we have the cross in our experience. We need therefore to deny ourselves and take up the cross and follow Jesus. There is a portion of the cross for each of us so that we can cross each one of us out. The cross is to deny self, put ourselves to death, and to apply the cross of Christ to ourselves all the time. Our fellowship is in our meetings, at our homes, and with God and Jesus all the time. We should flow as electricity, tuning into each other and Jesus. The Divine Fellowship corrects us, moulds us, and reconstitutes us. We enter into our spiritual being which causes a change in our being. Without the cross we have no release, freedom or liberty from the self. With no spirit or cross we cannot have real fellowship. When we are crucified, Jesus lives within us. This is the cross which we take to the Lord and to release our old self and to let Jesus into our well-being.

Growing in Life by Dealing with the Spirit

God's Spirit enters into man so he can be revived and uplifted and not to live by the Flesh and soul but in God's Spirit.

The person we are comes from the Spirit within us and releases our good intentions, keeping evil thoughts and filthiness away, so we can be cleansed and broken by the Lord, never proud or stubborn, but to follow Jesus throughout our lives into his Kingdom of sanctification.

We should never live in self-glory of ourselves, never boast or put down people, but to uplift each other, as we are not perfect on Earth but God is working every day to make us into his Bride and to eventually guide us into the Kingdom of his Heaven.

Dealing with the Natural Constitution in Order to be in Resurrection

To receive the cross we need to be crucified and the Old Man becomes the New Man. To receive the cross we need to apply our natural ability and what we are capable of is then touched by God. When we are regenerated we can then be transformed but still be natural. When we are built together we touch on the matter of being broken, and if we are not broken there can be no building.

We need our Old Man to be crucified, so that our sins no longer serve us as slaves.

God needs resurrection as after burial the resurrecting God brings the significance of death to the cross of Jesus Christ.

We should not put our trust in Satanic things, but in Jesus Christ.

We can trust in our Spiritual attainment, but this has to be terminated.

We can be conformed to the resurrection by living a crucified life in our Christian Life with Jesus Christ.

Being a Qualified Servant of God by Having the Complete Experience of a Called One

When you believe in Christ you have a Spiritual Father. We are nothing and have no reality without the Lord. The all-inclusive one is the one who comes to call us. We can be good like Abraham or neutral like Isaac, and Jacob the all-inclusive God. But God is our God whatever we are. God did not release Paul from prison, but came to resurrect him. God blesses each of us in the Triune God, with his riches, and enjoyment of his abundance, his love, and to gain more of him.

We can then be conformed to his image, the firstborn son of God. We can come to the full sonship.

God needs to do matching and cutting for each of us. We need to be willing to let God in and circumcise our natural life, then we can live by God's resurrected life, becoming useful in the hands of Lord Jesus and for the fulfilment of the Lord Jesus's purpose.

Our experience today should be with the Lord Jesus and his recovery.

Transformation for God's Building

We need to be fully enlightened and fully saturated with the thought that this Universe God is doing just one thing:- Building His Eternal habitation.

God has no interest in anything else.

For God to enter into each of us, he needs to mingle into us and into our Humanity.

We cannot be built up without God. Even if we could be built without God it would never be the Building of God.

God comes into the believers and to do this, incarnation is required, and the process of death and resurrection is required.

God needs us to build us up as a Spiritual building to express, represent God by dealing with Satan and to recover this lost Earth.

A Man of Power

In Acts, the Apostiles had God in them, first they prayed with God, then they worked with God. When we pray to God and our prayers are toward Christ then you will be heard.

As a Christian, we should live before God, but to also live in God, so we become one.

Our prayers are always with God inside us, he will guide us with the words, and while we pray uplift us into his Glory.

Prayer is for abiding with God. Our prayers are always with two friends, ourselves, and god.

We are not people who pray alone, God needs to be within us to guide and uphold us.

Words of prayer come from God.

God's Purpose for the Church to have the Divine Sonship in full through santification for the corporate Expression of God

God chooses his people for them to be made Holy, and to become sons of God, to Participate in Divine Sonship, and into Eternity.

God brings us into Glory, and this is what God is doing today for all of us.

We can become Christ's expression in full, in Glory, so we become the image of the Glorious Christ, and to make us into the Expression of Christ.

A Sister or Brother who cooks a meal for other Brothers, Sisters, is also dispensing the food Jesus provides to gain more of his Economy, and this way God is 'cooking' in the Church and for the feast not what the Brother, Sister prepared, but the laid table for the fragrance of Jesus for all of us to enjoy.

Correspondence

Sister Rosemary, Brother Chris, for you, and your son serving in the Army, as I thought that this would be very much received as of your concern and worries with your son serving and protecting others. May these words also protect each of you, and may the Lord Jesus be your son's guidance and protector in his troubled time, and also your troubled times with the worry of his service and the prayers of him returning safe to your side.

So, this is what I've found for you both to pass on to him, as long as you both do not mind.

Therefore, the peace accomplished by Christ on the cross is a firm footing, a firm foundation. As we fight against the evil powers, the peace Christ has accomplished is a firm foundation for our feet. To take part in the spiritual warfare, our feet must be shod with this firm foundation.

In the past most of us thought that the shoes of the gospel were for us to walk or run in our preaching of the gospel However, the firm foundation of the gospel of peace is not for running, but for standing. For running we may have a pair of lightweight shoes, but for standing we need a pair of sturdy shoes.

In fighting, the crucial thing is to stand. We must be able to stand and to withstand the attacks of the enemy. Those who are defeated will run, but those who are victorious will stand. As we wrestle against the enemy, we shall find that Satan does not run away. Therefore we need to be able to stand. Spiritual warfare is not a boxing match, but a wrestling match. If we would wrestle against the enemy, we need a firm footing. Hallelujah, in the Lord's recovery we have such a foundation. Because there are those who have their feet shod with the firm foundation of the gospel of peace, they can withstand any attack of the enemy. Because they have such a firm footing, nothing else can shake them. No matter what happens, they can stand and withstand in the evil day.

Usually peace is the opposite of warfare. When we have peace, we do not fight, and when we fight, we do not have peace. But here we fight with peace and in peace. We fight by standing in peace. If we lose the peace between us and God or between us and other believers, we lose the standing. Christ is the peace for us to be one with God and to be one with the Saints. This peace is the firm foundation that enables us to stand fast against our enemy.

Christ is the righteous element that covers us, and Christ is the peace that enables us to stand.

From Sister Elaine Day.

Remember also you're always welcome here for an evening or lunchtime meal. Just let me know when you are available, we enjoy your company a lot.

100 Years, and Ivy is still going strong.

You're a gem of a mother, and a great Mother-in-Law
You ask for very little, and you remember everyone's birthday and Anniversary as well.
You're a friend to everyone, from your Grocery Store to your Church People say a warm 'Hello' when Ivy comes to call
As a Mother-in-Law you're the best I could have
You're the great, and never small
Never been educated, but you've done us all proud
You've been a gem at accounting
Breakfast comes after your Church
Placing the Lord before your meals
Your devoted to your family, and devoted to your Lord Jesus
You, Ivy are a real treasure to behold
Putting many of us gathered to shame
Your easily pleased, a smile always on your face
Many lifelong friends have you had
And many are still around
William has been with you
Keeping you in order
So that you rest, unlike your daughter-in-law
Mavis, who charges around
But never stops, always working for the Lord
And just like you, her family as well.

This ditty comes from all gathered with our love
And Ivy, will there be another 100 years?
When we can all gather and celebrate some more?

Best wishes Ivy, from Elaine, David Day.
Enjoy your celebrations with the Lord and your gathered family & friends.

Dear Becky & Roy.

Here is a little something I've written for you both, hope that you like this.

We have known you for such a short time
But our friendship has blossomed with the Lord
We walk and talk him
We sing together our joy of his existence
And we eat and drink as one
Sorry about the gall bladder
But the fish I understand was fine
Hope the hedgehog makes a good journey
To be in a land where it is warmer, and away from the cold of his basket
Enjoy your bus cushion
A reminder of journeys to Tesco's and beyond
Romford will soon be a distant memory
Wait until you see a Nun
Before you venture to the other side
Best to go to Rome early
When there is only a faint hope of the bikers
No helmets, no manners,
Boy, you will enjoy it.
Just leave my favourite restaurant alone.
It is the one with the man who stands outside
Near to the Trevi fountain,
And if you do not have enough for his table
There's more money to be found in the fountain.

Then there is the Ice Cream shop
Remember to show David the ice cream in your hand
And when you return to Bower House
Bring yourselves and the memories
Plus of course bring Jesus with your travels
Then we shall wine and dine
But don't go down with a bug Becky
Because Roy will be so cross
As he will find a card
Which says no money included
Because it's been left in Rome
So enjoy your flight
And your stay tonight at the hotel
Don't eat the food on the plane
God knows where Becky will end up
Don't be alarmed Roy
If another hospital visit is due.
Safe journey to both of you
God Bless you both.

Samuel and Estella Donkoh

Here is a little ditty for you both
About a driving instructor, and a mad cap woman
Who needs so desperately some driving lessons
And, Samuel is the answer to her prayers for this task
But, before Samuel gives Elaine her driving lessons
He will certainly need his holiday with you Estella
And, in turn, Elaine will need her break as well
So, Samuel, please enjoy your holiday with Estella
While there is still hair on your head
And, please come back feeling very refreshed
And drive over to where Elaine lives
But, PLEASE, do not drive to Gallows Corner
EVER, at two in the afternoon
Best, therefore, to go at two in the morning
As there will be some roadkill then?
Plenty, that is for Michael Reddy
For the kitchens at Bower house
But, sadly, Samuel, there will be no roadkill for us three
As we would be in fits of laughter
Feeling so very sorry for the Brothers and Sisters
Not really knowing or understanding what Michael Reddy is
Dishing up
Deer, Fox, Rabbit, and maybe a badger or two?

Different dining then for those up at Bower
PRAISE THE LORD INDEED
And, besides the two of us Samuel, we shall need the infamous Back seat driver
As, no driving lesson is complete without one of these
So, dear Sister Estella, this is where you come into all of this
To let both Samuel and me know when you spot the roadkill?
So, we should forget about those MADMEN at the corner
And, beat this, Sister Estella, MADWOMEN on the kill?
But, somehow Samuel, after my first lesson
THERE WILL BE A MADMAN at GALLOWS CORNER
Sister Estella, your husband will by then should have no hair
So, before you both go on your holiday
Take plenty of photos of Brother Samuel PLEASE.
As you will see Samuel in the NOW and the AFTER if you see
What I mean
Samuel will be in shatters, gibbering like a nervous wreck
And, when he is tucked up in bed with you Estella
He will say to you.

'NEVER AGAIN ESTELLA, teaching YOU WAS BAD
ENOUGH, NOW I've passed another MADWOMAN,
   on the
Roads, GOD FORGIVE ME.
But, I hate to tell you, Estella, Elaine was right.
Look at my head, my HAIR HAS ALL GONE.

Lightning Source UK Ltd.
Milton Keynes UK
UKOW04n1334090215

245937UK00001B/15/P